Slavery in America

Marie Patterson, M.S. Ed.

Table of Contents

Slavery in the New World

Europeans first sent slaves to the Americas in the 1500s. The slaves did not have a fresh start like others that came to the new land. Instead, they began hard lives of **servitude** (SUHR-vuh-tood). By 1860, there were four million slaves in the United States. Most were destined to harsh lives with no rights and no choices.

▼ Slaves in the United States were finally freed in 1863.

Slavery: Nothing New

Slavery has been around for a long time. Long ago, there were no machines to help people get their work done. People who owned businesses and farms needed many workers to be successful. So, powerful people made poor people work for them. When the workers were paid no money, it was called slavery.

The settlers in the American colonies were no different. It was hard work settling new land. They decided to bring Africans to the colonies to help with the work. In the early 1600s, Africans were brought over as **indentured servants** (in-DEN-shured SIR-vuhntz). This means they were freed after working for four to seven years.

▼ African slave market

Triangular Trade

There were three parts to the Trans-Atlantic Slave Trade. Trade goods were shipped from Europe to Africa. Then, Africans were sent as slaves to work in the Americas. Finally, products from the Americas were shipped back to Europe.

▼ African villagers captured for the slave trade

African Traders

Slave ship captains got their captives from African men called traders. These traders had kidnapped their captives from villages around Africa. They sold their own people for guns, metals, or alcohol.

Soon after, the Trans-Atlantic Slave Trade began. Slave trade was a very **profitable** (PROF-uh-tuh-buhl) business. British and colonial ships traveled to Africa. There, traders picked up human **captives**. These men, women, and children had been kidnapped from their homes. They were put on the ships and taken to the colonies.

The Africans were very hard workers. They knew how to grow crops during hot weather and on swampy lands. The slave owners knew they could get rich off of this slave labor.

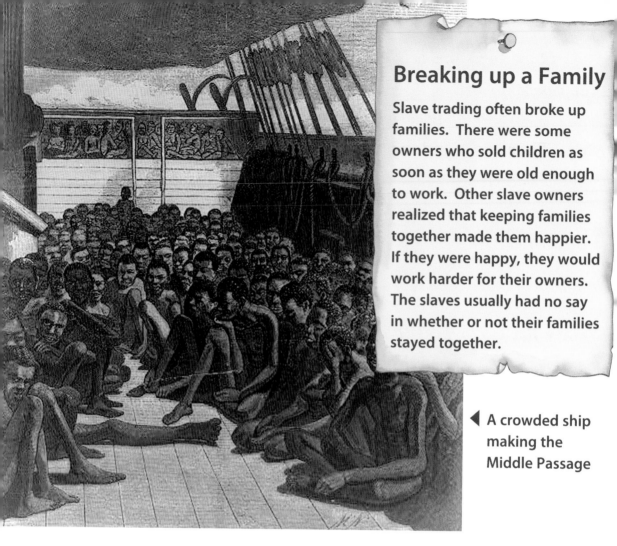

Breaking up a Family

Slave trading often broke up families. There were some owners who sold children as soon as they were old enough to work. Other slave owners realized that keeping families together made them happier. If they were happy, they would work harder for their owners. The slaves usually had no say in whether or not their families stayed together.

◀ A crowded ship making the Middle Passage

From Africa to the Plantation

The Africans came across the ocean on slave ships. This trip was called the Middle Passage. The traders wanted to make as much money as possible. So, they packed far too many captives onto their ships. They did not give them enough food or water. Many Africans died during the terrible journey.

Once the ships reached the colonies, the traders sold their captives. Sometimes, the Africans were sold at **slave auctions** (AUK-shuhnz). In a slave auction, the captives were lined up. Then, rich landowners **bid** on the captives to buy them. Whoever bid the most money owned the new slave.

Slaves were thought of as property, just like a piece of furniture or a horse. The owners could do whatever they wanted with the slaves. Once a **slave master** owned a slave, he could treat the slave however he wished. This meant slave owners could sell their slaves at any time.

The Kinship Network

Since owners sold slaves at any time, the slaves developed a kinship network. This meant that slaves at a plantation welcomed new slaves and took care of them. By helping others, they hoped that their kindness would be returned if their family members were ever sold.

▼ This scene shows a slave family being separated at an auction.

Slavery Grows in the South

The large **plantations** (plan-TAY-shuhnz) in the South required many workers. The plantation owners realized they could save money if they used slaves. A slave owner had to provide food, clothing, and shelter for his slaves. In exchange, the slaves did all the work on his house and farm.

Slave owners could also hire out their slaves to work for other farm and plantation owners. This was very profitable. The slaves received nothing for this extra work.

▼ Slaves using a cotton gin

The Cotton Gin

Plantations throughout the South grew different crops. Some of the most important crops were cotton, tobacco, and rice. In 1793, a man named Eli Whitney invented the cotton gin. This machine allowed southern farmers to produce more cotton. Cotton became very popular in Europe and the northern colonies. This caused slavery to grow in the South.

Fearing a Rebellion

As the number of slaves increased, the colonists feared that the slaves would revolt. So, the white owners became harsher in dealing with their slaves. Owners whipped and branded their slaves to make them afraid.

▲ This image shows a female slave being branded.

▼ Tobacco plants drying in a colonial barn

The demand for slaves grew as **agriculture** (AG-ri-kuhl-chuhr) expanded in the South. This caused slave trading to increase. In other words, the slaves helped make plantation owners rich. So, the owners bought more land and planted larger crops. Then, the owners needed more slave labor to work the land. It was a terrible cycle.

How Slaves Lived

A slave's day was 12 hours long, six days a week, all year. Slaves did anything that their owners wanted them to do. Field slaves did work such as clearing land, farming, and mining. Others trained to be builders and metal or leather workers. This was hard physical work. The women worked in the fields alongside the men.

▼ **Slaves returning from the fields at the end of the day**

Other slaves were house slaves. Male house slaves served as personal servants for the masters. Female house slaves served their mistresses. The slaves cleaned, sewed, washed clothes, took care of children, and cooked.

Slaves could not own anything or earn money. They could not even get legally married. Owners kept their slaves separated from other people. They wanted their slaves to be **isolated** (EYE-suh-late-ed). They felt that this was the best way to control the slaves and prevent escapes.

▲ Many slaves lived together in small cabins like this one.

Slave Culture

Slaves in the South developed their own special culture. Their culture included religion, folk songs, and dances. This lifted their spirits and promoted unity among the slaves. This culture is still studied today so that we can learn about the lives of slaves.

Born into Slavery

If a female slave had children, then her children became slaves as well. Slave owners expected the slave families to care for their own children. The owners wanted the children to grow up to be strong workers. These children would one day make money for the owners.

It was up to each mother to care for and educate her children. Mothers were only supposed to teach their children the skills they needed to work. Slaves were not allowed to teach their children to read and write. The white owners did not want the

Child Care

The young slave children stayed at home in a "nursery." Sometimes there were as many as 20 to 40 children in the nursery. Usually, slaves who were too old to work watched the children. In these nurseries, they did crafts, told stories, and played games. Does this sound like anything you did when you were little?

▼ An 1862 photograph of slaves next to their cabin

Day of Rest

Most slaves had Sundays off. They loved to spend time with their families. They enjoyed fishing, hunting, and wrestling. Some families would get together with friends and play the banjo, sing, play marbles, or even gamble.

▼ Slaves dancing and singing on their day off

slaves to learn anything that would help them work together.

During the day, most young slave children stayed with elderly slaves while the parents worked. Some babies would go to the fields strapped to their mothers' backs. Other babies were placed in baskets in the fields. Slave children had to begin working for their owners by the age of five or six.

Who Were the Abolitionists?

The Constitution of the United States was written in 1787. At that time, the leaders of the country debated slavery. Southern leaders convinced the others to keep slavery legal.

Soon after, leaders of the churches began to ask if slavery was right. The first group of people to speak out against slavery was the **Quakers**. They wanted to end all slavery in America.

Declaration of Independence?

Americans were very proud to have a special country. Here, people had control over their lives. They could make their own decisions. People expected "life, liberty, and the pursuit of happiness." It is hard to understand how a country that was so proud of earning its freedom could hold millions of people captive.

Famous Abolitionists

William Lloyd Garrison

Harriet Beecher Stowe

Frederick Douglass

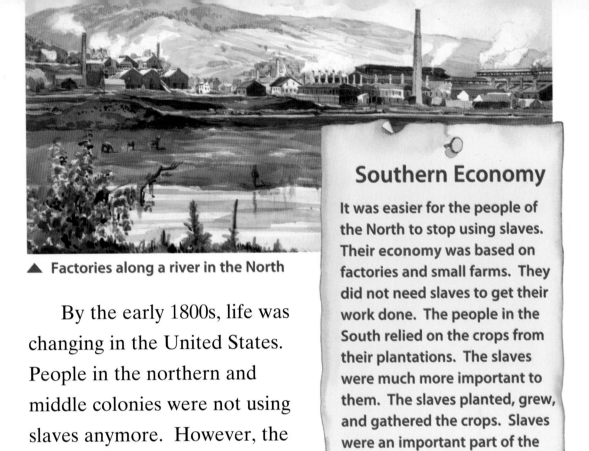

▲ Factories along a river in the North

Southern Economy

It was easier for the people of the North to stop using slaves. Their economy was based on factories and small farms. They did not need slaves to get their work done. The people in the South relied on the crops from their plantations. The slaves were much more important to them. The slaves planted, grew, and gathered the crops. Slaves were an important part of the southern economy.

By the early 1800s, life was changing in the United States. People in the northern and middle colonies were not using slaves anymore. However, the people in the South still refused to end slavery in their states.

Many people thought the South should be forced to stop slavery. These people were called **abolitionists** (ab-uh-LISH-uhn-istz). They thought that all the slaves should be free.

The abolitionists knew that they would face a fight in the South. Southerners would not want to end slavery. Most people believed that slave trading and slave auctions were the worst part of slavery. The abolitionists decided to attack that part of slavery first. After a long debate, it was decided that all slave trade in the United States must end by 1807.

▲ Slaves escaping on the Underground Railroad

The Underground Railroad

The Most Famous Conductor

Harriet Tubman was one of the most famous conductors on the Underground Railroad. She was a slave who escaped on her own. After she escaped, she returned to the South to help family members escape. Then, she made many more trips to help other slaves. She was brave and clever. She led more than 300 slaves to freedom.

Some slaves tried to escape from their owners. Most were caught and punished. A few were even killed. Escaping became easier when the abolitionists started to help. They organized an escape route from the South to the northern states and Canada. They called this route the "Underground Railroad."

Henry "Box" Brown

An antislavery office in Philadelphia, Pennsylvania, received a mysterious box. When they opened it, the office workers found a man inside. A slave named Henry Brown had shipped himself to freedom in a three-foot (0.9-meter) wooden box. The trip took more than 26 hours. What a great idea!

This Underground Railroad did not have train tracks like a normal railroad. It was a "railroad" because it had many stops on the way to freedom. It was "underground" because it was secret. A person who led a group to freedom on the Underground Railroad was a **conductor** (kuhn-DUCK-tuhr). The slaves who traveled the railroad were passengers.

If a slave wanted to escape, he or she would be contacted by an abolitionist in the South. This person would tell the slave where to go for the first stop on the route to the North. At each stop along the way, the escaping slave would be told where the next stop was. Sometimes slaves had to hide in trees, swamps, or barns. Often, slave catchers would be chasing after them.

Some abolitionists just provided information. Others hid slaves in their homes and fed and clothed them. A few acted as conductors. All of these people risked their lives to help others gain their freedom.

No Place in Society

Who were the free black people during the mid-1800s? Some of them were slaves who had escaped. Others were people who had been freed by their owners. There were even some blacks who had been born free. Most free blacks lived in the North.

Free blacks had a difficult time in white society. Many people who thought there should be no slavery did not think that blacks were as good as whites. These people did not want free blacks settling in the northern states. White Northerners felt that the free blacks would take their jobs.

Abolitionists discussed what to do with the free blacks. Some whites did not think the blacks could work well without

Who Was Dred Scott?

Dred Scott was a slave. During his years as a slave, he traveled quite a bit with his owner. He even lived in free **territories** (TAIR-uh-tor-ees) for a few years. This means he lived in places where slavery was against the law. With the help of some abolitionists, he sued for his freedom. He thought that he should be free since he had lived in free areas. In 1857, the case went all the way to the United States Supreme Court. Scott lost the case, but his case was very important in the years leading up to the Civil War.

Dred Scott

supervision. They also thought that blacks were unskilled. Abolitionist groups tried to organize schools to teach the blacks how to read and write.

One group organized efforts to buy land in Africa. They called this new colony Liberia. They planned to send free blacks to live there. They thought this was a kind plan, but most blacks did not want to go to Africa. They wanted a chance to make their way in America. They felt they had helped build this strong new country, and they wanted opportunities. Unfortunately, it did not usually work out that way. By 1850, only 10 percent of blacks in America were free. And, the ones who were free worked for less money than whites.

Fugitive Slaves

The Fugitive Slave Act was passed in 1850. This new law stated that any slave who ran away from his or her owner had to be returned. So, slaves who ran away to the North were sometimes taken all the way back to their southern plantations. This made life much harder for blacks everywhere.

◀ Some free blacks did return to Africa to begin a new country. These ships are arriving in Liberia.

The Struggle to Free the Slaves

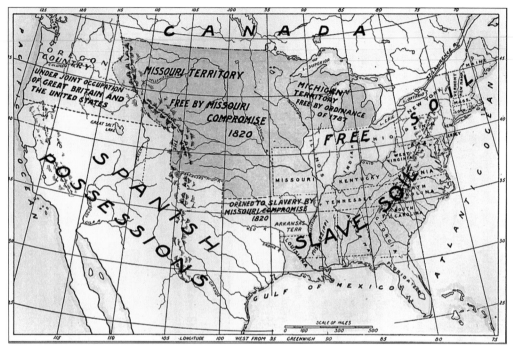

▲ Map of the United States in 1820

During the 1800s, many new states joined the Union. The abolitionists in the North did not want these new states to have slavery. The people in the South felt that settlers should decide on the laws for their own states. The Southerners did not want the free states to have more representatives in Congress. They worried that Congress would outlaw slavery altogether.

The conflict between the North and South grew throughout the 1800s. Soon, people were not just debating the issues; they were fighting each other over slavery.

William Lloyd Garrison

Arrest that Man

William Lloyd Garrison was a famous abolitionist. He published a weekly newspaper called *The Liberator*. In his newspaper, he wrote about how horrible and wrong slavery was. His newspaper became very important. Southerners disliked Garrison because of his beliefs. Georgia even offered $5,000 for his arrest.

By the end of 1860, Southerners were tired of arguing with the people in the North. They did not like that the Northerners told them what to do all the time. The South decided to leave the Union. This led to the United States Civil War.

Secession

South Carolina was the first state to secede (suh-SEED). Between December 1860 and May 1861, eleven states seceded. The word *secede* means to withdraw or leave a group. So, the southern states were leaving the United States of America. They formed their own country called the Confederate States of America. They even chose their own president.

Proclaiming Freedom

▲ Abraham Lincoln

What Is a Border State?

The Border States were the slave states that bordered free states. During the Civil War, most of these states remained with the Union. Delaware, Maryland, Kentucky, and Missouri did not secede with the other slave states. They stayed part of the United States.

In 1861, Abraham Lincoln became the 16th president of the United States. He believed that the main goal of the Civil War was to keep the country together. Lincoln thought slavery was wrong. But, he did not want to lose the support of the **Border States**. So, he had to be very careful about how he ended slavery.

In September 1862, President Lincoln announced the **Emancipation Proclamation** (eh-man-suh-PAY-shun prah-kluh-MAY-shuhn). This document stated, "all persons held as slaves within any State . . . in rebellion against the United States, shall be . . . forever, free." This is a formal way of saying that the slaves in the southern states were freed. The slaves in the Border States were not freed. Lincoln did not want the North to lose the support of those states.

President Lincoln was afraid that the Emancipation Proclamation would lose its power once the war was over. So, he worked to get the Thirteenth **Amendment** (uh-MEND-muhnt) to the Constitution written. In 1865, this law ended slavery in the United States. Americans could never have slaves again.

Slaves traveled a long, hard road from Africa to America. Some Africans never saw freedom again. Others fought every day of their lives to be free. Learning about slavery teaches us an important lesson. Everyone should respect the rights and freedoms of all human beings.

Amending the Constitution

Congressman Thaddeus Stevens wanted equality for blacks. In Congress, he fought for the Fourteenth Amendment to the Constitution. This law ensured that black men got the same rights as other citizens.

Thaddeus Stevens

Glossary

abolitionists—people who wanted to end slavery

agriculture—farming

amendment—a change or addition to the Constitution of the United States

bid—an offer of money for something

Border States—slave states that bordered free states

captives—prisoners; people who were held against their will

conductor—a guide; someone who led people out of slavery on the Underground Railroad

culture—the traditions and beliefs of a group of people

economy—the activities of an area that have to do with money

emancipation—setting free

indentured servants—people who worked for others to earn their freedom or to earn property

isolated—separated from everyone else

plantations—large farms that produce crops for money

proclamation—an official government announcement

profitable—producing a lot of money

Quakers—a peace-loving religion whose members opposed slavery

secede—pull out or withdraw from something; states leaving the Union

servitude—a situation where someone has no freedoms

slave auctions—public sales where people bought slaves

slave master—a person who owned slaves

territories—areas of the country that were settled by Americans, but had not yet joined the Union